How Katie Got a Voice

(and a cool new nickname)

by Patricia L. Mervine, M.A., CCC-SLP

Illustrations by Ian Acker

"How Katie Got a Voice (and a cool new nickname)" was written by Patricia L. Mervine, M.A., CCC, a speech/language pathologist and assistive technology consultant who has worked with students who have significant disabilities for nearly twenty years. She is the creator of the popular website, www.speakingofspeech.com, and the blog, www.speakingofspeech.blog.com, two tremendous resources for SLPs, teachers, and parents who support children with communication impairments.

Illustrations are by Ian Acker, a freelance artist and illustrator, who lives in Pennsylvania with his wife and three children.

Visit www.PatMervine.com for a Discussion Guide, activities, and Katie's Disability Etiquette video

Order this book online at www.speakingofspeech.com

Most Trafford titles are also available at major online book retailers.

Illustrations by Ian Acker

Printed in the United States of America.

ISBN: 978-1-4269-6649-1 (sc)
        978-1-4669-4704-7 (e)

Library of Congress Control Number: 2012911406

Trafford rev. 2/29/2016

 www.trafford.com

North America & international
toll-free: 1 888 232 4444 (USA & Canada)
phone: 250 383 6864 ♦ fax: 812 355 4082

To Marie Mark, my first and lifetime mentor in the field of augmentative communication. Thanks to Marie's direct intervention and influence, countless students have gotten a voice.

At some schools, kids try to fit in by being the same as everyone else. They dress alike and talk alike, and they don't have much time for kids who are different.

It's just the opposite at my school. At Cherry Street Elementary, the best way to fit in is to be different. Being different is way more interesting, don't you think?

All of the students, all of the teachers, even our principal and custodian, have nicknames that tell what makes each person unique.

For instance, there's our principal, Mr. Sipolski. Principal Sipolski is never still. He spends his days dashing around the school, greeting the students at the door in the morning, visiting classrooms in the afternoon, and joining in kickball games at recess. He has so much energy that he is nicknamed "Mr. Zip." Mr. Kennedy, our custodian, does such a good job keeping our floors shined and recycling bins emptied that we affectionately call him "Mr. Clean."

My fourth grade teacher is Mrs. O'Brien. She is always smiling (as long as we behave) and she really gets excited when her students work hard in school. "Oh, boy!" she cheers when we all turn in our homework on time. "Oh, boy!" she applauds when we bring in something interesting for Show 'n Share. "Oh, boy!" she smiles when she hands out a "caught being good" sticker to a student who helped another, even when he didn't have to. Can you guess her nickname? You are right if you guessed Mrs. O'Boy!

All of the students in my class have nicknames, too. When you know their nicknames, you also know what makes them different from everyone else.

Because he is such a good artist, Jose is called "Picasso."

Because Bonita always has her nose in book, we call her "Bookworm."

Bill "The Boot" is our class kickball star.

He scores in almost every game we play at recess.

Two of my friends collect things. "Penny" (really Pari) collects coins in blue folders. She tries to collect coins from every year, going all the way back to 1980.

"Bugsy" (really Brandon) collects dead insects. He pins them inside a box. Underneath he prints the insect's scientific name along with the date and place where he found it. He wants to be an entomologist when he grows up (that's the official name for "bug scientist") but I think he just likes to gross out the girls.

My good friend Tina has taken piano and cello lessons since she was three years old. When she's not playing an instrument, she's listening to music. And when she's not listening to music, she's humming -- sometimes even in the middle of taking a test! Her nickname is "Tunes."

We have lots of fun in our class, but nobody can make the class laugh as hard as Giovanni, "The Jokester." Even when his jokes are real groaners (and a lot of them are), we still have to laugh. He says it's all in the delivery.

And I guess I should introduce myself. My parents named me Miguel, but all my friends call me "The Punster" because I have a way with words. I don't like to brag, but I'm the one who thought up a lot of the nicknames. Most of the time the names come to me in a flash, but one time I was really stumped. Everybody was.

You see, a new girl moved into our school district. Her name was Katie, and she was not at all like the rest of us. For one thing, Katie was in a wheelchair because she had a hard time controlling the muscles in her arms and legs. She couldn't walk. She couldn't hold a pencil, and she couldn't feed herself. A woman named Miss Hanscomb stayed with Katie all day to help her with those things. Her job is called "Personal Care Assistant," or "PCA," for short.

Another thing you should know about Katie -- she couldn't talk. She could smile, and blink her eyes, and make a few sounds, but she couldn't say any words. She had a notebook with some pictures on each page. By gazing at the pictures, she could ask Miss Hanscomb for something to eat or drink, or to make a choice of movies to watch or places to go. Katie's eyes moved around a lot, but when Katie looked hard at a picture, Miss Hanscomb would know what Katie wanted and would say the message out loud. Without Miss Hanscomb to speak for her, Katie did not have a voice.

"Welcome to Cherry Street School, Katie," said the principal on her first day. "My name is Mr. Sipolski, but everyone calls me by my nickname, Mr. Zip. Everyone in our school is different in some special way, and everyone has a special nickname. Once we get to know you, you'll have a nickname, too." With that, he zipped Katie down the hall and into our classroom. Poor Miss Hanscomb had to run to catch up.

"Here we are, Katie!," boomed Mr. Zip as he pushed her into our classroom. "This is your new teacher, Mrs. O'Brien, but everyone calls her Mrs. O'Boy. I'm sure you'll find out why, about 20 times a day!" Everyone laughed, even Mrs. O'Brien.

"You'll have a wonderful time in the fourth grade!" With that, Mr. Zip winked, smiled, and zipped back down the hall. I hate to admit it, but we all just stared at Katie. I mean, we tried not to, but we never had a student like Katie in our class before.

"Hello, Katie! It's so nice to have you with us," said Mrs. O'Boy. She went around the room, introducing Katie to Picasso, Bugsy, Bookworm, Tunes, and the rest of us. It was Katie's turn to stare at us. I guess she had never heard such strange names before.

We all tried very hard to be nice to Katie. We tried to talk with her, but she really couldn't answer us. She would smile or blink or sometimes make a sound, but that was it. It was hard to know what to say to someone who couldn't talk back.

At recess, Bill The Boot and the rest of the class felt bad about leaving Katie on the playground, but how could she play with us when she was in a wheelchair?

Jokester told her some funny jokes (and a few groaners) that made her laugh, but she couldn't tell any jokes to him so pretty soon he excused himself and went to trade jokes with other kids. Katie couldn't paint with Picasso. She couldn't pick up coins or insects with Penny and Bugsy. And she couldn't play music with Tunes; she couldn't even hum.

The truth is, it seemed like Katie couldn't do anything without Miss Hanscomb, or "Miss Handy" as we called her, because of all the help she gave to Katie. She really was Katie's hands...and feet.... and voice.

I must say that this made us all feel pretty bad. One day a few of us stayed after school to talk with Mrs. O'Brien. "Katie is a nice girl, but she can't walk, she can't play, she can't even talk," we said. "We don't know what to do with her."

"Since she can't do anything special, I can't even think of a nickname for her," I added.

"Oh, boy," said Mrs. O'Brien quietly. "If you are feeling bad, imagine how Katie must feel. Let me see what I can do." We didn't know what she had in mind, but we could tell from her faraway look that she was working on a plan. We hoped it would be a good one.

The next day, we saw Mrs. O'Brien talking with the speech
therapist about Katie. The speech therapist's name is Ms. Markle
but everyone calls her Ms. Lips because she has all kinds of funny
red and pink lips all over her therapy room. She says the lips remind
her students to use their best speech. "Don't worry," said Ms. Lips.
"I have some ideas that might help Katie."

During the next few weeks, Ms. Lips took Katie to the speech therapy room every other day. Now here was a mystery we just couldn't figure out. Katie couldn't talk at all. Why would she go to speech therapy? Many students do go to speech therapy to fix certain sounds like "s" and "r" that might be hard for them to say clearly. Other students go to speech therapy to work on language and following directions and memory skills. Picasso goes to speech therapy because he stutters sometimes. But Katie wasn't going for any of those reasons. Why was she going to speech?

Well, we didn't find out until much later, but here's what was happening.

First, Ms. Lips gave Katie a switch, a big yellow plastic button with a cord attached. She put it in many places: on Katie's wheelchair tray, beside her head, next to her left knee, and behind her right elbow to see which position was best for Katie.

Katie could hit the switch in some of the places but not in others. She was best using her left cheek. With practice she got really fast! She also learned to use a joystick. It looked a lot like a joystick on one of my big brother's old video games, but instead of using her hand on the joystick, she learned to move it with her chin. It was hard work and made her tired, but she kept working at it and got better every day.

Katie discovered that she could do many cool things with the switch and joystick. She could play games in computer class and turn on electric scissors in art. But, very best of all, she could use a switch with a communication device to talk! Miss Handy said Katie's eyes lit up when Ms. Lips first showed her the device and all the things it could do. The communication device is a small computer screen with a bright grid of colored squares. All of the squares have words and pictures on them. Each square lights up in a row, one at a time. When the square with "drink" lit up, Katie hit her switch and the computer said "I want a drink, please" -- out loud -- in a young girl's voice! Katie was thrilled! She now had a voice!

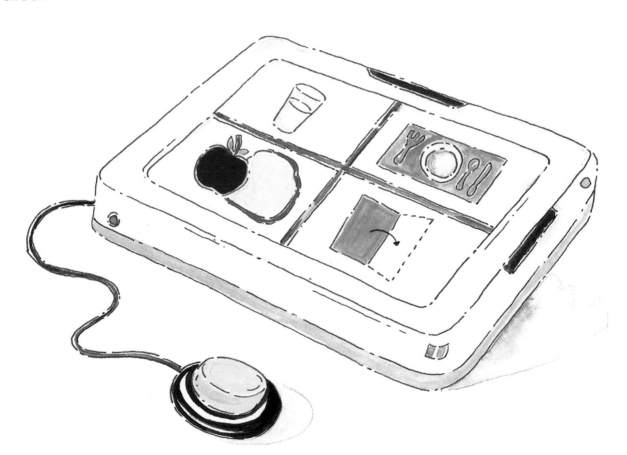

She and Ms. Lips practiced using the switch and the communication device for several weeks, but they kept it a secret from the rest of the class and even from Mrs. O'Brien, because Katie wanted it to be a surprise. More than anything, she wanted to hear a loud, happy "Oh, boy!" just for her.

After weeks of practice, Katie was ready. Miss Handy and Ms. Lips came into our classroom carrying all kinds of things with wires and plugs. They wheeled Katie to the front of the room and hooked up her switch to an MP3 player. Katie moved her head and music began to play. "Awesome!" whistled Tunes. "Katie can play music, just like me!"

Katie's switch was then hooked up to the classroom computer. A storybook appeared on screen. The computer read the story to the class and turned the page every time Katie moved her head. "Cool," yelled Bookworm. "Katie can read books, just like me!"

Then Katie changed the program on the computer and another amazing thing happened. The students stared at the screen as Katie began to draw! "Sweet!" called out Picasso. "Katie, you're an artist, just like me!"

Next, Katie's switch was connected to a small rectangular box with a screen. None of us had ever seen anything like this before. "This is called an augmentative communication device," explained Ms. Lips. "What does it do?" we wondered. We were about to find out. Katie carefully watched the screen as square after square lit up. Suddenly, she moved her head and we heard a voice from the device say, "Why did the chicken cross the road?" Jokester burst out laughing. "Hey, now Katie can tell jokes, just like me! But I'll have to give you some new material, Katie. Chicken jokes are the biggest groaners of all!"

Katie smiled, looked back at the device, and hit her switch again. This time the device said, "Do you want to see my collection of postcards sometime? I have one that came from China and another from New Zealand." "Yo, Bugsy," exclaimed Penny. "Katie is a collector, just like us!"

Again Katie stared at the screen and hit her switch. "Go, team, go!" said Katie with her device. "Hot dog!" hollered Bill the Boot. "Team, it looks like we just got ourselves a cheerleader!"

We were all so excited to hear Katie's new voice and to see all the cool things she could do with her switch. For the first time in her life, Mrs. O'Brien was surprised beyond words. She stood by her desk, watching silently and smiling, as we all crowded around Katie.

"Is there anything else you want to say, Katie?" asked Ms. Lips.

Katie nodded. Then she stared at the screen for a long time, choosing words carefully to make a sentence. When she hit the switch for the last time, the students heard "I want a nickname, too." Katie looked right at me, and so did everyone else. Wow, a nickname for Katie. I had nicknamed nearly everyone else in the room but here was a real challenge, and the time had come to face it.

I gathered my classmates to one corner of the room to talk over the possibilities. "When we first met Katie, we knew she was very different, but we didn't think she could do anything special. To be honest, we didn't think she could do anything at all. But now with her switch, she can do so much. She can even use her switch and that device to communicate."

Then, in a blinding flash, it hit me! "That's it!" I whirled around to face Katie. "From now on, you will be called CommuniKate!"

"OH, BOY!!!" whooped Mrs. O'Boy. She clapped her hands and did a happy dance with Ms. Lips and Miss Handy. The whole class cheered. Even Mr. Zip dashed in to celebrate Katie's new nickname.

And CommuniKate smiled her biggest smile ever.

The End

People who have disabilities may be different from you in some ways, but in many more ways they are just like you! And just like you, people with disabilities want to be treated with respect. How should you do that? Here are some rules of good manners for you to follow.

1. When you see a person who has a disability, look right at the person and smile. Don't stare and don't look away. How would you feel if someone either stared at or ignored you?

2. When you talk to a person who has a disability, do not shout or speak to him like someone who is much younger or not as smart as you. That would be very insulting!

3. When a person who has a disability is with a personal care assistant, a sign language interpreter, or other companion, be sure you speak directly to the person, not the companion. If you do talk to the companion, don't talk about the person as though he isn't there.

4. If you are talking for a while with a person who is in a wheelchair, sit down or try to position yourself comfortably so you are both at eye level.

5. Some people with disabilities have service animals, usually dogs, who are trained to do special tasks for their masters. They may be cute and friendly, but don't pet them without asking permission. Service animals are "on the job" and should not be distracted or disturbed.

6. Some people who have disabilities use computers and other interesting equipment called "assistive technology." These are not toys. This equipment is often fragile and expensive, and it is very important to the person who uses it, so do not touch or play with it.

7. There are many things you can talk about with a person who has a disability, like sports, movies, school, and the weather, but it is not good manners to ask questions about the person's condition unless they bring up the subject.

8. A "visual disability" means that the person does not see well. It is helpful to tell the person who you are when you approach her. "Hi, Jenny, it's me, Joe!"

9. Some people are Deaf or are "hard of hearing." When talking with a person who has difficulty hearing, always face them directly so they can see your mouth as you speak. Speak clearly at a slightly slower rate, but do not shout.

10. Some people have a hard time speaking smoothly or clearly. This is called a "communication impairment." If you don't understand a person's speech, don't pretend that you do, as this could cause misunderstandings. It is okay to ask the person to say it again, or ask if he can write it down, or tell you in some other way. Just don't rush the person. Be patient with someone who uses a communication device, too. Let him know his message is worth waiting for.

11. Even though it might seem like a nice thing to do, do not automatically help a person who has disabilities without asking first. Say "Do you need help with that?" If the person says yes, ask what you should do. Just like you, people with disabilities want to be as independent as possible.

12. Always focus on the PERSON, not the disability! While it might be easy to see what the person can't do, look closely, get to know the person, and you will see all the things he or she CAN do. As the students in this story discovered, despite her challenges, Katie was in many ways just like them.

Since we are all the same inside, that brings us to the simplest and most important rule of all: Treat people who have disabilities the same way that you would want to be treated!

Printed in the United States
by Baker & Taylor Publisher Services